NATIONAL
GEOGRAPHIC

T0069730

Jeans

From Mines to Malls

PATHFINDER EDITION

By John Micklos, Jr.

CONTENTS

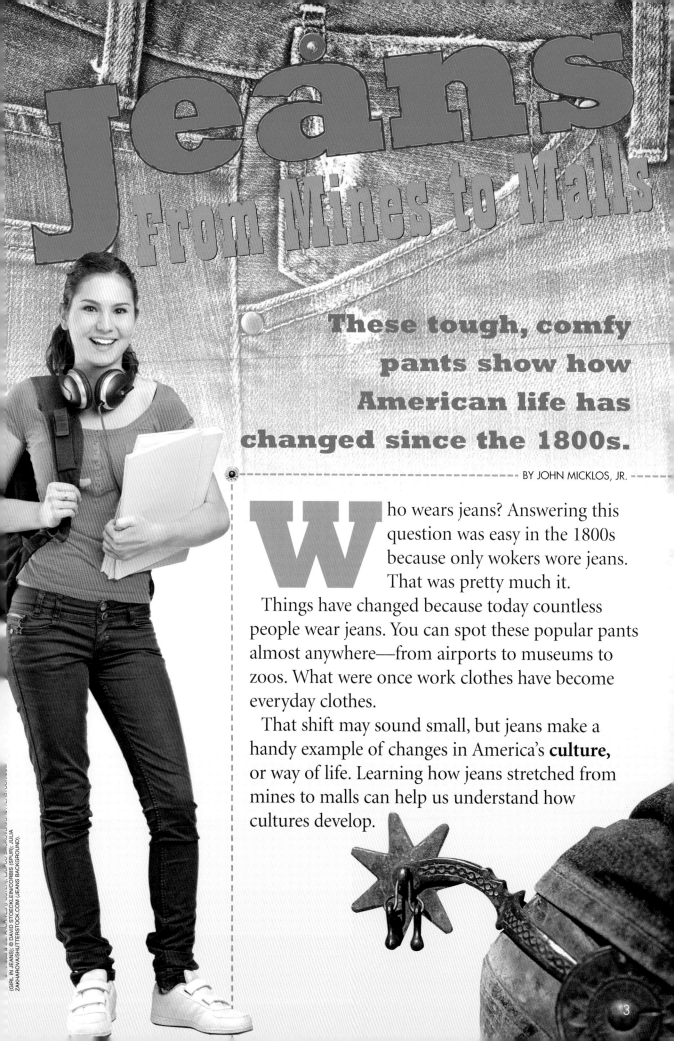

Jeans
From Mines to Malls

These tough, comfy pants show how American life has changed since the 1800s.

BY JOHN MICKLOS, JR.

Who wears jeans? Answering this question was easy in the 1800s because only wokers wore jeans. That was pretty much it.

Things have changed because today countless people wear jeans. You can spot these popular pants almost anywhere—from airports to museums to zoos. What were once work clothes have become everyday clothes.

That shift may sound small, but jeans make a handy example of changes in America's **culture,** or way of life. Learning how jeans stretched from mines to malls can help us understand how cultures develop.

A Riveting Idea

Our story begins with Jacob Davis, who was a tailor in Nevada during the 1870s. Some of Davis's customers kept ripping their pants pockets—and complained about it.

Pants tore a lot in the Old West, actually, because miners often stuffed rocks or gold nuggets into their pockets, and the weight was too much for most clothing.

Davis came up with a simple solution. He added copper **rivets**, or bolts, to the corners of the pockets, and the new pants were amazingly strong. They became an instant hit.

Now Davis had a new problem.

That Was My Invention!

Davis feared that other tailors might steal his idea, so he wanted a **patent**, which is a special government document. A patent gives an inventor the sole right to make and sell a new invention. No one would be allowed to copy Davis's pants until his patent expired in 1891.

Golden Opportunity. *Miners flocked to California after gold was discovered there in 1848. Needing tough pants, they loved denim.*

But Davis didn't have the money to file the necessary papers with the U.S. Patent and Trademark Office in Washington, D.C. Then he thought of Levi Strauss, a successful businessman in California, who sold cloth to many tailors—including Davis.

Davis wrote to Strauss, inviting him to be a partner in applying for a patent. Strauss accepted and on May 20, 1873, they received U.S. patent 139,121 for "Improvement in Fastening Pocket-Openings." Then they got busy.

Tough Pants, Tough Jobs

The two men set up a factory in San Francisco. It produced "waist overalls." That's what jeans were first called. To make the pants, workers used **denim**—a tough fabric made from cotton.

Miners loved the sturdy and comfortable pants. Then cowboys started wearing them, too. Jeans were perfect for riding horses and working on the ranch.

Early ads (page 2) stressed the pants' toughness. Pictures showed hardworking men—and just men because women generally didn't wear pants until much later. Besides miners and cowboys, there were jeans-wearing carpenters, railroad workers, deliverymen, and more.

Jeans on Screens

The popularity of jeans owes a lot to another invention from the late 1800s—movies. Inventor Thomas Edison opened the world's first film studio in 1893, and just ten years later, the United States alone had some 10,000 movie theaters.

Movies were a huge part of American culture during the 1920s and 1930s. Going to the movies offered a cheap escape from life, especially during the hard economic times of the thirties.

Watching films, people saw cowboys—in jeans. Americans who'd never worn jeans for work began wearing them for fun, and in 1935, Levi Strauss & Co. introduced jeans for women.

Fashion Model. *Popular actor James Dean—and his jeans—appeared in* Giant, *a 1956 film.*

Jeans Go Global

Then came World War II. The United States entered the fight in 1941. American soldiers and sailors went all over the world, and so did their jeans. The troops often wore them when not in uniform.

People in other countries soon noticed—and wanted—those comfortable, casual pants, and that's just one example of how the war spread American culture to other nations.

Jeans won even more fans during the 1950s. James Dean, Marlon Brando, and other popular young actors wore them—in movies and in real life. So did rock idol Elvis Presley. Before long, young fans were wearing jeans, too.

Jeans were almost a uniform for many young Americans in the 1960s. Denim and long hair became signs of social protest in the sixties, which was when people started to speak out for changes in laws and society.

Women's Wear. *During World War II, men went off to fight, so women worked in factories—and in jeans.*

Old Is In. *Clothing companies work hard to create jeans that look like they've been hanging around for ages.*

Big Business

Eyeing jeans' popularity, the fashion world saw a chance to make money. The result was "designer jeans." They hit the stores in the 1970s, and these new jeans had fancy stitching, fancy labels, and fancy prices. They became popular with people of all ages.

To get Americans interested in jeans, manufacturers spend millions on **marketing**, which is what businesses call the effort to sell something. It often includes research, print ads, and radio and TV commercials.

Jeans makers need to know what customers want—and don't—so they hire marketing experts to run focus groups. Those are gatherings at which people talk about a product and explain why they would or wouldn't buy the item.

It All "Ads" Up!

Stores today sell many kinds and colors of jeans, so each manufacturer creates advertisements to show how its brand special and set apart from the rest.

You won't see many miners in today's ads. Instead, you'll find famous people and beautiful models because the goal is to make buying jeans seem like an easy way to feel like a star.

All this marketing pays off, because in 2001, Americans spent about $13 billion on jeans, and those people didn't just buy pants. They also got a chance to step into history.

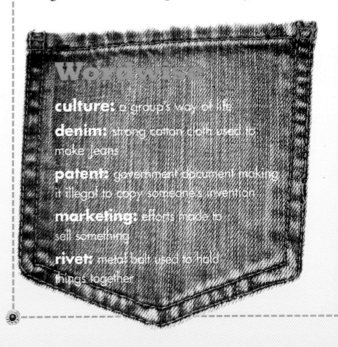

Wordwise

culture: a group's way of life

denim: strong cotton cloth used to make jeans

patent: government document making it illegal to copy someone's invention

marketing: efforts made to sell something

rivet: metal bolt used to hold things together

6

Ads: Best Sellers?

When was the last time you bought jeans? Did you really need a new pair, or did you just want the latest style? People buy products for many reasons. Advertisers target them all, and that's why there are so many different kinds of ads.

Copywriters, people who write ads, choose their words carefully. With just a few words, they have to get you to buy something. Take a careful look at this imaginary ad. Then create one of your own!

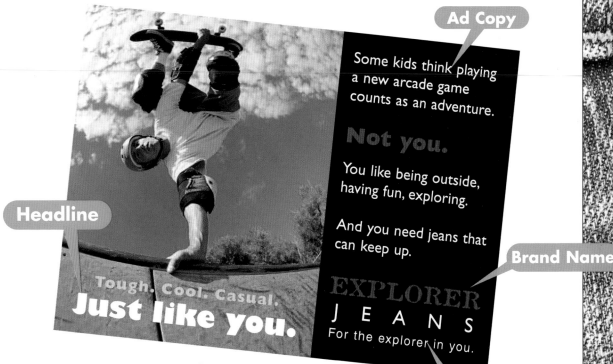

Reading an Ad

- Whom does the ad target?
- What is this ad's message?
- Do the words match the picture?
- How does the ad try to persuade people to buy a product?

Writing an Ad

1. Pick a product to sell.
2. Identify your target audience.
3. Give your product a brand name.
4. Make up a short slogan for your product.
5. Choose a magazine in which the ad would appear.
6. Decide what kind of picture the ad would show.
7. Create a headline to catch readers' attention.
8. Write ad copy that persuades readers to buy your product.

Fabrics From Nature

Jeans and other clothes are often made from natural fabrics. The materials used to make these fabrics come from plants or animals. Check out the fabrics on this page to see how they are made—and what makes them naturally great.

Cotton

Making Cotton Cotton grows on plants. At harvest time, fuzzy white balls cover the cotton plants, and workers pick these balls of cotton. Then the cotton is spun into yarn. The yarn can be used for knitting, but it can also be woven into cotton fabric.

Look and Feel Cotton fabric is soft to the touch. Some cotton fabrics are thin and lightweight, but others, like denim, are thick and strong.

Cotton Clothes Casual clothes are often made of cotton. T-shirts, shorts, jeans, skirts, dresses, and sweaters are examples of cotton clothes.

Silk

Making Silk Silk is made by an insect called a silkworm. The silkworm wraps itself with a long string of silk thread. When it is done, workers unwind the string from around the silkworm and then weave it into silk fabric.

Look and Feel Some silk fabrics are thin and cool, while are tightly woven. The thick weave makes them heavy and warm.

Silk Clothes Fancy clothes are often made of silk fabric. Popular silk clothes include dress shirts, blouses, suits, and neckties.

Wool

Making Wool Wool is a sheep's thick layer of curly hair. Sheep farmers cut off the wool about once a year. People then pull and twist it into yarn. People can knit the yarn into clothes, such as sweaters. The yarn can also be woven into fabric.

Look and Feel Wool is warm. Some wool fabrics are thin and smooth, but others are thick and rough to the touch.

Wool Clothes Winter clothes are often made of wool fabrics. Wool is good for sweaters, pants, jackets, suits, and socks.

Dry on the inside.
Waterproof fabrics
keep people dry in
wet weather.

otton, silk, and wool are natural fabrics, and they are great for many kinds of clothes. But natural fabrics have their share of problems. For example, they don't protect you from a cold wind.

So people have found ways to improve on Mother Nature. They have invented new kinds of fabrics.

One of these fabrics is called nylon. Nylon is made from plastic and it blocks wind. Nylon fabric is thin, so it doesn't weigh very much, but it is also strong and won't rip easily.

This does not mean that nylon is "better" than natural fabrics. It is just better at some things. For example, nylon is better at blocking wind.

Staying Dry

Another problem with natural fabrics is that rain soaks through them. They get wet and heavy. So people have invented many fabrics that block water and keep you dry.

It's no surprise that waterproof fabrics make good raincoats and jackets. What is surprising is how some of these fabrics work.

Would you guess that one waterproof fabric actually has many tiny holes in it? Most waterproof fabrics are airtight to keep the water out, but many of these fabrics also trap heat.

The solution is a fabric with holes. The holes are small enough that water drops can't squeeze through. Yet they're big enough to let your body heat escape.

Improved

Warm in the Cold.
New fabrics let people explore the coldest places on Earth.

Holding Together

People have found some great ways of improving fabrics, but sometimes people steal their best ideas from nature.

That was the case when an inventor named George de Mestral created Velcro. It's a plastic clothes fastener. One side of Velcro is covered with tiny hooks. The other side has tiny loops. The hooks connect to the loops to keep on clothes and shoes.

How did de Mestral get the idea for Velcro? One day he went for a walk, and some burrs got stuck to his pants. He looked at the burrs. They had tiny hooks that latched onto loops in his pants fabric. De Mestral imitated the hooks and loops to create Velcro.

Improving Fabrics

Each day, people are finding ways to make new kinds of clothes. These inventions don't just give us new kinds of fabrics and fasteners. They change the way we live.

New fabrics don't just protect us from wind and rain. They give us new opportunities. Today, people can explore the world's coldest places. New fabrics also let people explore outer space. Adventures like these would be impossible without the right clothes.

Does this mean new fabrics are better? Not necessarily. It all depends on what you want to do. Natural fabrics are good for some activities. Man-made fabrics are good for others. The choice between them is up to you.

Jeans

Try these questions on for size to see what you've learned about jeans.

1 Why did Jacob Davis add rivets to pants?

2 How did Levi Strauss help make jeans popular?

3 What role did Thomas Edison play in the popularity of jeans?

4 How does marketing affect what people decide to wear?

5 How have people improved some kinds of fabrics?